School

by Linda Cave
illustrated by Gary Undercuffler

Pre-Decodable 5

Bothell, WA • Chicago, IL • Columbus, OH • New York, NY

MHEonline.com

Copyright © 2015 McGraw-Hill Education

All rights reserved. No part of this publication may be reproduced or distributed in any form or by any means, or stored in a database or retrieval system, without the prior written consent of McGraw-Hill Education, including, but not limited to, network storage or transmission, or broadcast for distance learning.

Send all inquiries to:
McGraw-Hill Education
8787 Orion Place
Columbus, OH 43240

ISBN: 978-0-02-146205-6
MHID: 0-02-146205-4

Printed in China.

10 11 12 13 14 DSS 27 26 25 24 23

the  and

boys girls

the  and

tables chairs

the  and

school students